1,/ Tests

Luke Emmett

Leafe Press

Published by Leafe Press
Nottingham, England.
www.leafepresspoetry.com

Copyright © Luke Emmett, 2024. All rights reserved.
Cover artwork © Rupert Mallin, 2024. All rights reserved.
ISBN: 978-1-7397213-1-2

Acknowledgements:

The poems "Weight" and "Word Full" were first published in Tears In The Fence 76. Thanks to David Caddy and his editorial team.

Cover artwork: "Over the Horizon" (ink and wash collage) by Rupert Mallin
Used with kind permission of the artist

1,/ Tests

Stuck

Movement; a spasm
of laughter accusing

uncared. Taste
pain to bodies, touch

on coupled scissor,
reddish, bent.

Delusional

For liminal counter,
the heart shd lack
what it pertains to,

vision.

Nightshade Hymns

Bloody poison of milky red,
berry

    shade
toward sleep and move route,
spit in basin; check image,

has passion again, unfamiliar.

Roam

to going,
have holy,
profane.
Be torpid,
the rind
of pace.

Nembutsu

A gutter spits, pan
is quick toast; child
rise soon, routine
to diary repetition,
repeat learned phrase,
scuffing butter.

Proximal

The mesial surface
(pointing toward)
of canines, distal
(pointing away from)
surface, incisors;

    hands poke,
in pine rubber, busy
to midline face.

Calm

Day, today is sweating upon
his closed window she brushes
almost clean,
in panicked equilibrium,
to see it again, again.

Buttons

For a short thread string to
cloth, the button I've kept
has three holes, shines.

Continue to pick the loose
matter; I hope for visitors.

Wrench

Having undergone
a strange feature of wrench,
      lightly I,
very light, return; a stroll.

The world in...

Day with/out golfing
was wasted.

Storms kept possible
movements steep
and vertiginous.

Heave (why any labour
will move) component:
week one.

Rub

Jacket on chair

still there. I will

wear it;

it creaks.

Out

The scope of my scream
-- will autocomplete --
the scope of my scream.

After the event he

wept

wept

wept

wept

wept

Jesus wept

wept

soften my tears

wept

Place

to Seishin

Flood in order; time
is ten gulls by mossy bark.
A prayer will save.

Ear

I've compared seldom

lyric conscious to mutable
task, to cut stone,
the vestibule
sits with in awkward tomb.

Anew metro

my memory conveys some song
that had no sense –
a pattern to love's pretence.

Weight

Were we lovers, I'd asked
— recalling our September
and her sip of water —
she wanted water
— escaping our soaking;
first love dead.

Word full!

She found all words
in resonate method,
so left it spread,
forever septum drip.

At least...

I have almost plastic
artificial gin and
rank morning alone
having vomited twice
and wasted neither time,
then conspire to again.

That Hobgoblin,

he's a real card isn't he?
What does he say?

NOTHING IS FOREVER

Milton Keynes UK
Ingram Content Group UK Ltd.
UKHW051154240624
444546UK00007B/103